I0199456

Journeys Through Prairie and Forest

Poetic Essays On the Big Questions of Life

Volume 5 — Babylon's Fall, Eden Restored

Journeys Through Prairie and Forest

Poetic Essays On the Big Questions of Life

Volume 5 — Babylon's Fall, Eden Restored

Volume Five of a Seven-Volume Set

By Paul W. Syltie

Also by Paul W. Syltie

The Syltie Family in America

The New Eden: Millennial Agriculture,
a Key to Understanding the Kingdom of God

How Soils Work: a Study Into the God-Plane
Mutualism of Soils and Crops

Understanding God's Government,
With Contrasts to Satan's Governmental System

The Three Edens, the Story of God's Universe, Earth,
and Mankind in Conflict With the Adversary

Pathways to Joy in Marriage;
Live This Way and Happiness Will Pursue You!

The Bridge to Eden, the Arduous Passage
From This Age of Chaos to the Next Age of Perfection

Journeys Through Prairie and Forest
Volume 5. Babylon's Fall, Eden Restored
by Paul W. Syltie

Publisher: IngramSpark

Editor: Paul Syltie
Editorial Assistant/Proofreader: Sandy Syltie
Photographer: Paul Syltie
Interior Design/Composition: Greg Smith
Cover Design: Greg Smith

ISBN-978-0-9980254-4-5

Printed in the United States of America

To my wonderful wife of 53 years,
and to our children and grandchildren who are the hope of the future.

Table of **CONTENTS** Volume 5

All photos have been taken by the author over many years.

PREFACE

WHO AM I?
WHY AM I HERE?
WHAT IS MY DESTINY?

These three questions have haunted the lives of virtually every thinking person on earth to one degree or another. They point to the very heart of our existence, and to our ultimate value, our worthiness to exist. Are we products of evolution from a primordial sea-soup, without any defined purpose in being here, or are we creations in the image of a Creator whose plan for us transcends our understanding?

The answers to these simple but profound questions dictate our decisions day by day, and ultimately the course of our careers, our friendships, our marriage partners, and how we interact within our families and communities. In many ways these answers direct our career pathway through life, and most assuredly influence our joy and fulfillment in everyday living.

I am stepping out by claiming that I have found answers — sound answers — to all three of these questions, and I am audacious enough to suggest that they are correct answers. They agree with what I understand is Truth, which is rooted in the great eternal God who made all things, and who sustains all things through the Word of His power and revelation.

But there the simplicity ends. My audacity has led to great conflicts with the realities of a corrupted earth and universe … a corrupted human race that clings to existence day-by-day upon the whims of weather and cooperation … neither of which often prosper to any race's benefit. We are always only weeks away from famine upon an earth that so often insults the farmer and gardener with drought, floods, heat, frost, or tempest.

As a farm boy raised close to nature, I have been so often forced from my peaceful home into the prairies and forests, the lakes, streams, and oceans of this wide earth to regain my bearings, to restore hope and gratitude, and to reset the pathway ahead when darkness threatens to overwhelm me. To leave the sterile unease of concrete jungles and flee to the forests and prairies of sanity has become a habit over the years — an addiction, one might say — and with that flight has emerged a continued stream of verbal expression that has leaped from my fingers. I cannot explain why, just that I must do it.

So … here is a collection of some of those writings expounded over the years, some of them clearly poetic, and some of them bordering more on short essays. I attempted some way to categorize them to make them flow, but they have defied clear organization; each item is too complex to easily arrange in a coherent order. Thus, I have let them fall where they may within broad categories, and have applied pictures I have taken through the years to emphasize the messages. Photographing nature has been a passion much of my life; these images speak louder and more eloquently than my words.

I hope you enjoy these messages, and are brought into a closer association with the Creator as a result so you will be able to answer these three big questions a bit better yourself. Let us walk together through the prairies and forests of our land, our beautiful, God-given land that speaks to us so eloquently if we will but open our ears and listen.

IATA
LOT
SKIE LINIE LOTNICZE
SALOMON

Airplanes and Airports

Airport Madness

Mind-threads rest uneasily in places such as this,
Men and women of all extractions and persuasions brought together into an unintelligible mob,
Their fears, doubts, perversions colliding on all sides
Like an undisciplined troop of children — though these demons are unseen,
Careening throughout this time and space uneasily,
Seeking peace but finding it not,
Awaiting extinguishment in the face of righteous men's dreams
That ever throw down the bulwarks of evil,
And still the storms of lost soul's tempest.

Airports of Loneliness

Airports of loneliness, passengers of despair,
Quietly suffering their prison-term a-flying through the air.
Terminals of quiet waiting, anxious eyes daring not to meet
The eyes of other wary, weary warriors of flesh, discrete
As unholy flesh may be … waiting, waiting, wishing
For bucolic realms of cottonwoods, winds, and fishing
For souls of the lost 'midst towering ruins,
Of war-weary wayfarers through history strewn.

Warsaw, Poland. *Airplanes move people quickly from place to place over the earth, beyond the capacity of the human body to thrive, and typify the impatience that so characterizes modern society.*

Chapter 1 Airplanes and Airports

Airways of Grief

Engines of man's invention growl and rumble their way along concrete runways,
Erupting in flaming anger and vengeance as silver machines take to the air,
Soaring where flesh was never intended to ascend,
Forsaking fair mother earth and her soothing lullabies far below,
Impatience prevailing above the sanity of longsuffering,
Earth's supple scents forgotten among the rigors of city's steel and concrete,
Compassionate sun and ozonic pure air lost to industry's heated blast,
Pressed outside consciousness of daily enrapturement
By gray walls, nonsensical conversation — filling in time —
Serving men's ideals taught by other men, schooled in self …
Forsaking the Maker of their own fragile frame,
The One who pleads daily with all men
To acknowledge truth and plant feet firmly upon supple soil,
Far below the maddening skyways of jet planes' roaring thunder.

Flying

Chasing the sun at breakneck speed,
Prolonging the day, doubling its sway,
Distressing man's body, spirit, and soul
That he might reach his destination
So quickly,
Oblivion his fortress and stay,
Going nowhere faster and faster.
Oh, how did we get this way?

Chapter 1

Airplanes and Airports

Silver Bird

Airborne … floating effortlessly among clouds …
Like spirit, with wings unfurled,
A lumbering bird lost to technology's emulation of God
So shiny, so sleek,
Yet but a tin foil visage
Of that spirit reality soon to be.

The Airport

Unhappy souls, these airborne gents,
Bereft of solace, lost of sense,
Fearful eyes, afraid to gaze
On fellow traveler's joyless haze.

So friendless lie the desperate halls
Arranged in concrete's hardened calls,
Forgiving no one 'midst the hustle
Of streaming droves of endless bustle.

Children holding daddy's hand,
Thrust so far from nature's land,
Awestruck through the hallways tall,
Hoping roaring planes won't fall.

It is a paradox, this deed,
A technologic quest for speed,
To traverse distance far beyond
Man's healthful harmony with God …

But on he goes despite the pain,
Such suffering confused with gain,
Until the Adversary lies
In chains, when human tears shall dry.

Central Iowa. *Modern day Babylon is characterized by hardness and brutality, typified by this monstrous tractor that tears and pulverizes the soil with the cold, iron implements it pulls across the land. "And the fourth kingdom shall be as strong as iron, for just as iron hammers and breaks everything in pieces, so shall it break and conquer every kingdom" (Daniel 2:40).*

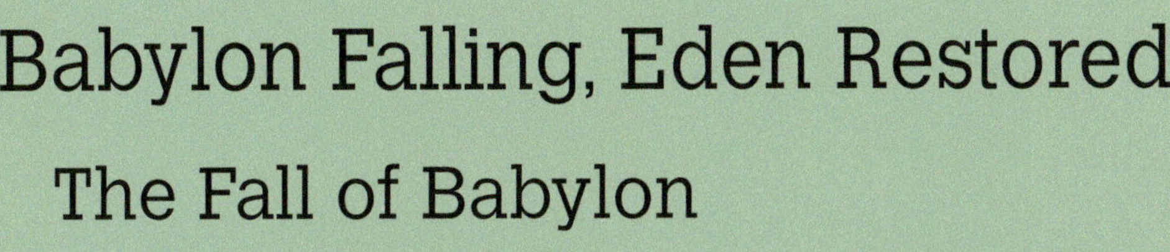

Babylon Falling, Eden Restored

The Fall of Babylon

Late autumn breathes warmly over the south Texas plain …

> Skies blue and cloudless,
> Soft breeze of Gulf's wings caressing oak leaves yet clinging
> To gnarled, low-slung warriors on rocky hills;
> Grasses bereft of seed, yet stretching in prayer
> Above rocky, leaf-strewn hills and vales …
> Frost having signaled next generation's release to slumber
> Within winter's cocoons of sequestered life.

All lies peaceful, all lies pleasant, jays and warblers gracing my ears.

Yet, deception lies within man's realm:

> Poisoned dreams, men preying on men,
> Fortunes made and lost in gambling markets — Wall Street —
> Usury untold, draining life-blood of struggling soldiers,
> Tables bare, homes taken by force,
> Mantles laid down before magistrates …
> Hopes and dreams laid low before Babylon's lawyers,
> Her judges feasting on the spoils …
> Land bought and sold, homes frittered away
> By usury, taxes, lies, fraud … blood, tears.
> Men prefer death to life,
> Forgetting that God will reward evil for evil
> In His due time … in His due time.

Continued on page 6

Babylon Falling, Eden Restored

Continued from page 5

Peace of nature belies the disaster soon to erupt
When spiritual gifts are traded for physical gods of pleasure,
Pillars of gold, silver, steel, stone … glitter, and pride.
Very soon, yes very soon the Eternal will strike terror within the
hearts
Of pleasure seekers, kings, and great men of the earth
Who substitute material splendor — passing fancy — for true wealth,
Spiritual gifts: humility, joy, and faith.
Very soon will fall the pride of nations,
Armaments of people led to death by leaders deceived by
soothsayers,
Babylon and her merchant ships extracting wealth and vitality
From the hungry, poor, and homeless.
Very soon the debacle shall cease.
I feel it almost here, the downfall of Babylon.

Prepare the way, prepare your hearts,
For Babylon, the mother of harlots, is falling!!!

A Better World

Earth's subtle face speaks softly to me;
So deftly she hides her secrets that we
Must speak through our beautiful language of friends;
"What is it", she sighs, "you seek 'midst my winds?"

Oh, show me a carpet of moss smooth and free
Upon which my feet may run painless with glee,
And let the morn's fragrance be pungent and fresh,
As once when a child I first smelled your soil's breath.

Continued on page 9

South Africa. *Typical of Babylon and all of the earth's land since the fall of mankind in the Garden of Eden, thorns and thistles were prophesied to compete with man's efforts to feed himself within an ecosphere that suddenly became competitive and predaceous.*

Egypt. *A hot, barren, formidable desert replete with garbage strewn from inconsiderate passersby has become the remnant of mankind's tenure on the land, the end result of his exploits while raping the soils of their native worth year after year. Kingdoms rise and fall as they either carefully tend the land, their most precious resource, or mine it for short-term gain.*

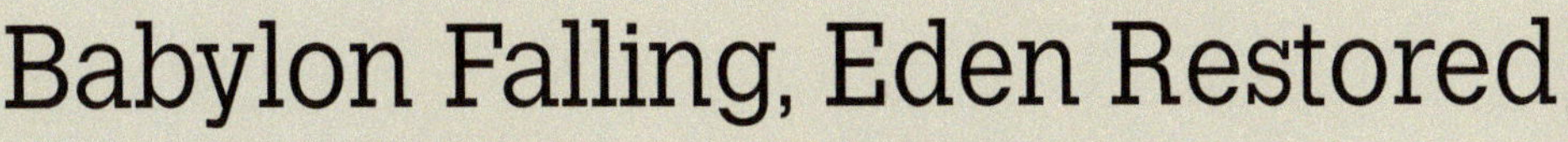

Babylon Falling, Eden Restored

Continued from page 9

Cause fruit trees and herbs to adorn every road
Along which I travel, beside each abode
Sequestered amongst flowered plain and treed valley,
Beside living waters where joyful hearts dally.

And let your harsh deserts turn green and refreshing,
Your winters forever to summertime's blessing;
The lion and rattlesnake harmless and friendly,
Storm's brutal ravages pleasant and kindly.

Earth smiled at me, her secrets abiding
Within her shrewd bosom as precious gems hiding
Their glorious luster for but a short date;
"All these I'll give you, and more … just you wait."

Age of Iron

Age of steel, iron, brass, titanium, refined metals of earth's artisans,
Plunging mankind headlong toward industrial machinery, capitalism, incorporation,
Paper wealth flourishing amidst vigorous trading of nations and their shoppers,
Merchants of the earth granted free reign to flow goods far beyond porous borders,
One-world visions bright within their carnal minds, rife with material pleasures —

Trading of gold, silver, spices, cattle, grain, machines …
And the souls of men.

Continued on page 10

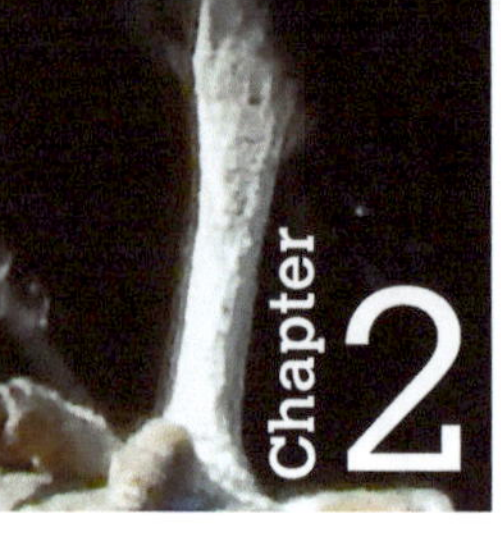

Babylon Falling, Eden Restored

Continued from page 9

Age of iron, age of hardness, age of venality, breastplates of stainless steel
Sodden with sultry schemes of artificer's vain imaginations, forged in compassionless heat
As Vulcan gets his way … for a time, a very short time
Before the elect seize the world with great force,
And engines of iron melt away before living trees and flowers, beating hearts of men and beasts,
An earth exuding life abundant, death vanquished amidst the broken, shattered tools of burnished metals.

Babylon Is Falling!

Babylon is falling, is falling!
I glance at my watch and gaze into the mirror: it seems to be time, does it not?
A few worried wrinkles grace my forehead … and only a few short years ago,
When life seemed oh-so troubled, so intensely convoluted as I strode through fields and forests, searching for solace …
But no one would tell me; I had to search alone the depths of twisted culture …
Far from cities of commerce — pushed ever to the margins — whose wanton games I could not understand …
Did not want to understand … but in restless abandon the Life-Giver laid Truth gently at my feet,
And I could not turn away.
I felt the heat of city's corruption, the wayward chaos steaming forth as a furnace, flung across the land of promise,

Continued on page 13

Wagoner, Oklahoma.
One of the most repugnant of all creatures, the turkey vulture, sits awaiting its next meal of decaying flesh, a symbol of death and destruction for all peoples and nations as they continue on their pernicious ways that lead to destruction and obliteration, as predicted by the sages of old.

NABORS
728

Babylon Falling, Eden Restored

Continued from page 10

Tainting this fertile field with rills, turning that bubbling creek to a raging torrent,
The wages of the workmen in the fields held back by fraud, the gleaners of grapes gaunt with hunger and perplexity …
Nineveh's son drawing nourishment from the soil surrounding it as a malignancy, distressing field and flock amongst the hinterlands.

Babylon is falling, is falling!
The haunt of every wicked and terrible bird of prey.
Oh, my eyes rain tears upon the land of promise; my heart cannot be consoled for her unceasing torment
Thrust across the land of Israel's beauty, now swarming with Gentile masses streaming across undefended borders,
The hedge of God's protection knocked down to the ground,
Souls of the destitute from desolate nations turning inward, usurping sanity,
Breaking through the bounds of civility … dark men driving airplanes like missiles towards Babylon's core,
Her very soul and spirit, her faceless corporate substance borne of profits and margins … love of money …
Madmen, madmen, madmen! Stalkers of the innocent and defenseless on bright, sunny days.
I cringe with horror as skyscrapers burn, and then collapse, a ghastly pall of billowing smoke and dust overspreading tentacles upon Manhattan,
Humanism infecting schools and homes — God's sovereignty denied — while homes neglect the commission to teach the children:

Continued on page 14

Pritchett, Texas. *Symbolic of the hardness and rapacity of modern Babylon — in the template of the Roman Empire — a drilling rig bores 24 hours a day deeply into the rock strata underlying the eastern Texas hills, in search of gas to power the economic engines of modern society, based upon finite fuel sources and uncertain riches.*

Chapter 2

Babylon Falling, Eden Restored

Continued from page 13

Young and old forsaking their God, their Creator, for fear of governments of men …
And few are those who stand in awe and wonder of the maelstrom approaching,
The hideous face of the Adversary rearing his ugly presence amongst the fertile lands of Israel.

Babylon is falling, is falling!
"And except the days be shortened there should no flesh be saved alive,
But for the elects sake those days shall be shortened",
But no one seems to care, to turn to his Creator and admit his errors,
As the few who have a voice and speak the Truth are blasphemed for "ill timing,"
Their voices stilled by the champions of political correctness, their spines as weak in moral fiber as their listeners …
And no one dares admit that their evil is begetting curses.
No one dares to tell the truth about himself.
No one.
The pain hits too deep, and the change required too great; let the good times roll, for God does not see my sin, neither is He good or bad.
So the righteous hide, and are comforted as they look upward, and take heart in the assurance
That their salvation is near, so very near …
And their own lives, and the lives dashed to bits in airplanes, or in collapsed buildings,
The lives of those lost in automobile crashes, in wars past and future, or in suicides and horrible murders …
And the lives lost to aging from the sin in the Garden — all of us —
With the unimaginable suffering of countless billions throughout history who grieve and moan from malnutrition, disease, and fear
From droughts, floods, storms, volcanoes, insect plagues, pandemics, and war,
But mostly from corrupt and heartless governments of men, and the Adversary who rules through them …
Will all be made right some fine day …
Not too long from now … yet each in his own order …
For indeed …

Continued on page 15

Babylon Falling, Eden Restored

Continued from page 14

Babylon shall fall, shall fall!

Then pirates, terrorists, revolutionaries, and murderers will face their fate,
Even as I and everyone else must meet theirs …
But I pray that the wanton, misguided souls of humanity will be privy to true joy for just a little while,
For I believe that then they just might choose to live.

Death to the Beast

"Worship the Beast!" cried young soldiers strong,
While hoarding their booty amid the huge throng,
Whose death-throes moaned endlessly on through the night …
"Those miserable creatures of patience we spite!"

Onward the vessels plied dark churning deeps,
Rounding Cape Horn, cargo oily which creeps
To feed the glib Monster — of steel, brick, and gold,
Seeking to stuff within all it could hold.

Gaunt workmen — foreigners strange to this shore —
Heave toilsome burdens to even the score
The Beast says these poor souls must pay for their works …
Lost men of Israel in whose hearts lust lurks.

"Work on, you strangers … we'll scatter your pride!"
Shouts on the Beast and its huge host worldwide;
A fathomless monster of dark, filthy deeds,
Of whoredoms and blasphemy … demonic creeds.

Continued on page 17

Santiago, Chile. *The vanity of mankind knows no limits. Skyscrapers loom up over the business districts of cities scattered over all the earth, as if with one voice proclaiming the dominance of Mystery Babylon the great so that all people might bow down to the idols of stone and steel*

Babylon Falling, Eden Restored

Continued from page 15

Some few on their foreheads, nor on their right fists
Possessed fatal waymarks which countrymen list
As reasons for losing the safety these few
Now cherish in silence, their deeds clean as dew.

The Beast bellowed blaringly on through the night,
Its horrible deeds hid for fear of day's light,
While genocide, carnal entertainments and gold
Furnished delights for the reveling fold.

"Come on, join our fun; come and dabble in blood!"
Shouted the monster while chewing its cud …
Of men's dreams and hopes which the vanishing few
Now gasped in despair with this sickening view.

The sheltered encampment of saints in haste rose
The morning this Beast's whole domain was to close,
And prayed that such vengeance, its deeds should deserve,
Might somehow bypass blinded men whom blind serve.

Yet, breach must meet breach, all breaks even, we're told,
As humble commandments when broken must hold
The seeds of eventual repayment in kind,
Like gravity drawing huge planets, to find …

That entropy of matter, where all degenerates
Onto a constant plane of sameness energy equates …
In like kind so with spirit laws, whose glowing flow of fire
Engulfs all deeds, thoughts, words of man through good or bad desire.

And the Beast was found dead, with not a tear shed
Among the saint's camp from which all sin had fled.

Chapter 2 Babylon Falling, Eden Restored

Destined for a Fall

A world caught up in selfish ventures crass,
Uplifting men, not earth's and man's Creator,
Consigned to things and wings of silver air-birds,
Destined for a fall, eternal prisons.

Doom Coming to Earth's Destroyers

On all sides stress mounts
As the righteous seek shelter from the approaching storm,
And find that light shines brilliantly upon them,
Illuminating them to all the earth.
Men grow brutal, without natural affection, seeking for themselves,
Forgetting gentleness, honor, selflessness, mercy, and forgiveness.
The forests and prairies take on a grayish, dismal cast
Amidst the droughts and floods, acrid smoke and tainted air
Of nations bent on war, arming themselves at the Destroyer's behest,
Forgetting the One who made them.

Roar of cities — autos, trucks, planes, men — reaches up to the heavens,
Wreaking pain upon the ears of righteous men,
Casting despair on all, tearing minds asunder
While the untainted bear their burdens bravely, quietly,
Amidst the devastating rancor enveloping hopes and dreams.
Tears flow freely among the just, such heartache they must bear,
For a little while — a moment —
While the crisis passes over,
And they alone are granted solace and protection
From death's clear warning … presaging life's dominion throughout the universe.

Babylon Falling, Eden Restored

Chapter 2

Earth's Rest

Earth's rest …

That final heaven …
Disintegration of human intention …

Ordered image of God
Covers dust under feet trod,
While into heaven rise
Spirit realm's prize!

Eden Restored

And Adam said, "I surely shall not die
From one shall bite of forbidden fruit;
So luscious it looks, so sweet and supple."
One bite, death struck …
Life's course towards Hades wended its way
Through ages hence to war, calamities, disease, and death.

And Adam gasped at what he had done,
So vicious and destructive a course he had begun …
Error upon error bequeathed to his sons henceforth.
He dared not speak, so deep his grief,
Bitter tears upon soil breeding thorns and thistles,
Clay once fit to form God's image,
Now noxious, yellow and sterile, stricken with death.

Continued on page 20

Babylon Falling, Eden Restored

Continued from page 19

Some years later new fruits sprang up where never before seen,
From the very places the tears had fallen.
Adam was no more, but his children laughed for joy,
And played upon the fertile clay beneath their feet,
The moss and thick grass tickling their toes,
A valley lush and green winding endlessly to the horizon
Of Eden's revived kingdom.

Just One More Creature

One day from the valley there arose
A mighty creature, huge and cold,
Smelling of dill pickles, scales on its hands,
Reeking of vengeance with thick slimy strands,
Of rancid black noodles as hair dangling there,
Atop its huge head like a haystack ascare.
One beady eye glaring slowly about,
Two arms, two legs, huge and hairy and stout,
Shaking the earth with each plundering step,
Knowing all evil, no tears ever wept.
Destruction of all was its terrible game,
Fine weapons shrugged off from its cast iron frame,
Casting despair through each planet it tred,
Tearing down limbs, towns, huge cities left shreds.

Continued on page 22

Sinai, South Dakota. *The restoration of Eden can be likened to a flower that blossoms in the midst of a plain and featureless place, placing beauty and fragrance where once was hardness and ugliness ... which is the character of this modern day Babylon.*

Chapter 2 Babylon Falling, Eden Restored

Continued from page 20

Then from the abyss rose the huge roaring beast,
Teeth gnashing, arms swinging wildly, "What feast,
Would this creature make of the terrified world?"
Asked newsmen, known critics, wise men's tongue's unfurled,
For short would the time be that life would exist
Should long this great creature in freedom persist.

With one mighty bound from the vale it did leap,
Far over the chasm on crude, slimy feet,
Yet landing so nimbly one mile from the town —
New York was its name — it blinked madly to sounds
Of shoppers and traffic that 'round its feet flew,
Not seeing the hair, slimy feet, but a few,
Kind tourists who snapped funny pictures of that
New plastic display, kind of jolly and fat;
Or true wise men gazing with awe at the sight,
In fear that disaster should come from this plight.
They turned not their heads, not a word they could say,
But watch, pray, and hope it would soon go away.

Now even the roars of the great creature died,
Between the tall buildings, beneath which men cried,
So loudly he raised his great hands to his ears,
And pointed his eye elsewhere — lesser to fear.
For him? Fear? Such nonsense, for all were afraid,
Of past plundered cities and whole countries slain.
Yet yonder its sight wandered only to see,
An endless expanse even it would agree,
Would waste its great hulk, for beyond every hill
There stood hundreds more of the dark, shabby shells.

Continued on page 23

Babylon Falling, Eden Restored

Continued from page 22

One moment it stood there, at peace with itself,
But next panic shook it, the first ever felt
Within its great frame, what a shudder it was,
For earthquakes were felt from Detroit to Madras.
Now once more it bounded to rid it of pain,
By-passing the valley from yonder's lush plain,
To find simple peace as in ages before,
When last it had scrounged man to leave his hopes sore.
But here too the cool lakes had turned hot and thick,
From cities so mindlessly grimy and sick.

The monster now sickened, its scales turning green,
Its hair hanging limply, a now silent scream,
Turned to retreat to its home in defeat,
A now contoured valley where fat golfers greet.
With heavy steps dragging the creature slumped down,
To read a large billboard of one Texan's town,
Far off to the east where the ocean is blue
Where manger dogs' choices know just what to do.

So eastward it rumbled, whole towns falling waste,
But solace it needed, so onward it paced,
Until at the doors of a domed building there,
It mumbled these words, "Help poor me, I need care."
"You wait, son," they answered, as tongues rattled on,
Raising more taxes, not questioning wrong,
Until from pure boredom the huge creature yawned,
And withered and died on the president's lawn.

Ukraine. *Like a gorgeous sunrise behind a complex of belching factories of Babylon's industrial complex, so will the next age arise and overspread the entire earth, remaking it into the Eden that it ought to be for the abundant living of all the earth's inhabitants.*

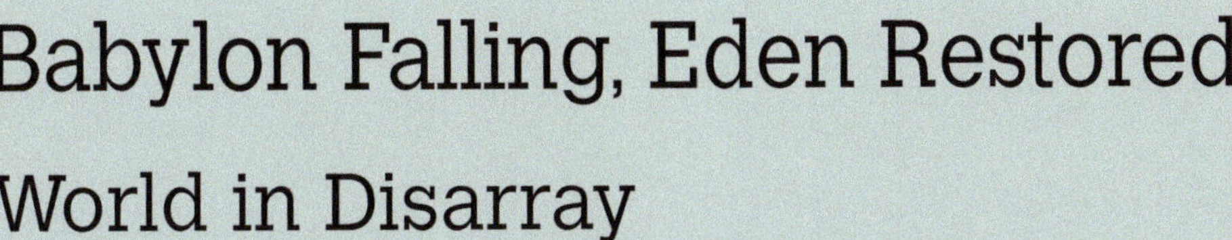

Babylon Falling, Eden Restored

World in Disarray

Homes of masses quietly resigned to slavery's task,
Stoop in fearful sighing 'neath their burdens dimly cast
Beneath long smoky shadows, city's skyline, factory's din,
Hope declining each long day through dark rewards of sin.

Skies so murky — where went deep blue hues of yesterday?
Storms of blazing fury throw their bolts … then melt away,
While rains in distant heartlands fail the seeds that farmers sow,
Or overwhelm the land as ceaseless torrents overflow.

The wife in city's prison casts her family's care so bleak,
Food bereft of value grant them illness, minds so weak
That self-styled leaders trample over kith and kin relentless,
Grasping for control of contrite hearts conceived so senseless.

Wandering 'cross the fruited plains and sprawling watercourses,
Tourists ply their belching autos much like unleashed horses,
Knowing not which endless road their roaring beast should take,
Seeking wholeness, finding life's lost fragments still opaque.

Winds still blowing, oh, so blowing, 'cross this land of plenty,
Idol's hewn on every corner, crossroad, mansion, shanty,
For a people glazen-eyed enamored with such pleasure
As the soul's imagination can in fullness measure.

Christmas cheer in mindless fear the masses fear to waver
From the common mantra sung, such greed and lust to savor.
Sabbath's call to restful worship cannot reach the throng
Overcome by things and idols shrouding truth's love song.

Calling to Eden

Future Dreams

Lying in the midst of pain God's servants ponder reasons for
This presence amidst the forest's shade, this place of torrid summer's pain.
Indeed the Lord will prosper him who lives in pleasure free from sin,
But why to receive the prize of worldly goods and storerooms full
Must such pain be endured to live this life of constant overcoming?
So clear the answer springs to mind: "That you must never learn to love
A culture fraught with wickedness, with sickness, death, and mindlessness.
This is a visage caught in pain, of suffering, unending stain,
Of life to life, and death to death, of hopes abounding smashed before
One's dreams should rest in this poor world, but rather in next worlds unfurled.
Indeed I shall in patient silence await this aeon's passing violence."
On to visions painted vividly in my youthful dreams discretely.

Life Recast

Whom does He call as servants of His way,
These humble men of flesh lost wholly to decay,
Death hanging 'ore their heads, ripped glibly from far lands,
Thrust into virgin shores of promise, Canaan's glorious strands?

Lost souls seeking foundations, contentment lost, abandoned,
Left far across the sea, rudder and anchor upended;
Quiet desperation stealthily stalking souls longing for peace ...
Unable to quench the heartache of mooring lost, released.

So when at last His call goes out these flustered souls dumb-founded
Look up and see a bright light beckon ... and cling to life rebounded;
Native lands and ways recast into total revision,
New kingdoms viewed in silent awe, new hope with soul's decision.

Sinai, South Dakota.
Like the message of trumpet-like daffodils sounding out their message of hope, peace, and light to the nations, so will be the institution of the new Edenic age when the reinstitution of beauty, abundant life, and love finally replace the rapacity and carnage of 6,000 years of war and suffering.

Tucson, Arizona.
The incredible beauty of the coming age cannot be fathomed by our limited minds, and restricted experiences during our short lives here upon planet earth, but our futures will be brighter and more fulfilled than we can possibly imagine, like a gemstone comprising the New Jerusalem.

Calling to Eden

Life's End

Life, be kind to me, your slave in bonds of courage,
Drifting swiftly amongst the ruins of Eden's demise,
Filling time's draught with tokens of endeavor …
Yet knowing not their ends, for I first must end before such fruits are fully ripe.
Life, deal me out your treasures,
That as I am but a vapor, that appears for a while, and then vanishes away;
Yet when all is done and I am gone
You may say of me when I repose in Zion's gates,

> "My Son, how well you have done!
> The assault was brutal, but you have won
> The contest, casting our Adversary's works asunder.
> Welcome to My world, where none of us shall henceforth blunder."

Shall my children, grandchildren — hope of eternal generations — cry in vain
For forefathers lost, my footsteps erased amidst earth's shifting sands, never seen again?
No, I think not in vain, for whence does love find its end?
As knowledge, tongues, and prophecies pass away,
Yet never shall the righteous intent of the chosen ones be deposed.
Failings we have, stumblings a-plenty, but stand we shall.

> In living each day, as humble flesh,
> That life's endless morrows might ever refresh
> The oft-burdened hopes of a joyous mind,
> Intent upon doing great works meek and kind.

Continued on page 30

Chapter 3

Calling to Eden

Continued from page 29

So swiftly flow the days, blending into the heavenly cosmos,
One speck of nothingness, it seems, against the blackness of never-ending suns
and galaxies;
Yet the battle I wage proves each thought, word, and deed to transcend the mere speck
that I am,
Visible in brilliance to the Creator of all I see …
The One who shall raise my worth and zeal to all eternity.

Made for Better Worlds

Torrid blasts of desert's wind flash harsh across my face,
Here amidst the toil of summer's unrelenting place;
Gazing over hills half-baked, whitened by the sun,
Eyes can hardly tolerate the hurting brilliance …
Not that light is not my goal and symbol of all good,
Which my mind's eye strains to see, if indeed it would.

But I know in Adam's realm 'twas easy for the eye
To cast its gaze upon such mountains, hills, and misty sky,
For the waters high above their stately presence gave
A light subdued for man to view all things in pleasant haze …

Not in squinting, stressful glimpses causing pain and toil,
Nor in such extreme exposure that one's skin should broil,
Or wrinkles mar this glorious creature made in His own image,
Created for an ageless life, no death to mar his visage.
No scorching heat to sear his soul, nor frost in winter's season,
Should strike this God-plane son of flesh designed for any season.

Yet with sin came down the waters stored above earth's heaven,
So we live in rank delusion caught 'midst death's dark leaven.
Oh, that soon would come the time when waters stored below

Continued on page 31

Continued from page 30

Would wend their way through titan forces upwards, then to stow
Their life-bequeathing shield so that these wrinkles soon would go
The way that evil deeds must flee from earth's bejeweled face,
Renewing life where once was death … where squinting finds not place.

Out of the Desert

Once alone in a biting desert land
I looked far into the distance,
With nothing but hot, shifting sands before me.
Water was nowhere, nor food to sustain me
During the long journey through this dry and thirsty land.
Onward I plunged into the great unknown,
Not knowing my course, for few were the signposts
Amidst the shifting sands of that blazing desert.
No help reached out from anyone,
For vacant and bereft of all life was this forsaken place.
There was no hope to survive the rigors
Of dry, blasting, hot winds searing my face,
But onward I trudged despite the odds of survival …
And on and on my weary footsteps strode
Upon hot and joyless places.

Then, when all hope had evaporated into the hot wind
I reached up for a hand
That quietly grasped my own,
And led me so softly but swiftly
Into a rich and fertile, well-watered realm,
The like of which I had never seen,
An Eden upon the earth, awesomely beautiful,
Filled with summer fruits and the Tree of Life.
The Eternal called, and I came to His feet
In a nick of time, just before time itself
Threatened to cease her patient vigil.
I cried with my brothers,
Now healed amidst the springs of Living Water,
Arriving as out of nowhere at my side
When I needed them most.

Chapter 4 Captivity, Freedom, Marginalization

Down But Not Out

I am tired …

Like an elk tracked relentlessly by hungry wolves,
As a tern embracing stiff gales on his oceanic flight,
Like a leaf torn and ragged, fluttering to earth …
Helpless, tossed into a mass of brown and green,
The sea of humanity;

I am lost …

The spoils of peacetime wars spitting fire ruthlessly about my head,
Burning pride and hope amid the quagmire of lust and jealousy;
Formless monstrosities — cities of asphalt — cry as trackless deserts

To their forlorn captives, sallow and pale,
Gasping with disease — of mind and body —
The politician's gameplay,
Of crackling jets and wretched rivers;
Stolen food of helpless farmers, oblivious to their charade in history's annals of false economy — efficiency, efficiency — more, MORE!

I am desperate …

For a world of peace, PEACE … real joy and kindness.
I loathe falsehood … and mirrors which unveil my own stains.
Yet for God's outstretched hand I would be one of them,
Though tired, though lost, though desperate,

Continued on page 34

Dubois, Wyoming. *Like a mountain capped by a pure white cloud, so does true freedom envelope the minds and hearts of those who are committed to a life of purity and lawful living within a world filled with temptations to do otherwise.*

Captivity, Freedom, Marginalization

Continued from page 32

Yet hoping beyond hope for vistas clear and pure, grasses green and
clean, pristine and simple … beautiful;
A sky of azure blue against distant storm's darkening ominous power,
The trills of songbirds unimpeded by industry's din,
Vistas clear to shimmering, warm horizons, crystal streams glinting …

So soon, so soon to arrive.

Exiled

Removed to margins, saints subsist among the clefts and rocks
In far-flung lands, as exiles bound to caves where silent flocks
Of patient prophets agonize in prayerful search for truth
Amidst world's night, this blackest hour, blind men insane, uncouth.

Fair earth reels like a dying orb, hurled deftly, far in space,
Few souls alive, most fearing to step out of bounds to face
The truth, its insecurity: tradition's sodden graves,
Abode of earth's destroyers … Babylon, her sons, her slaves.

Among the dead the living dwell, God's joyous exiles fair,
Austere of homes, stripped clean of earthly plunder lying there,
Which serve the dying, wand'ring whims of Babylon's last stand …
Their names inscribed in Zion's Rock, their longed-for final land …

And earth finds no abiding place
For exiles born of truth and grace;
Among their brethren yet they fight
As guiding lights towards Zion's height.

Death Valley, California. *Like a grinding desert landscape where rain seldom falls and hardly a thing can grow, so is the life of the captive to the transgressions of a world lost to hedonism. The plants that do grow last for only a season, and become dried up and gnarled as a forgotten relic.*

Chapter 4 Captivity, Freedom, Marginalization

Final Peace … and Beginnings

Within this aging world of confusion and despair
I find true rest and peace, but not just anywhere,
While striding down high roads, or soft and hidden places
Nowhere fellow men don upcast, joyful faces …
Or speak righteous words, principles rare and clean
Caring for feelings of this God-made being.

So in quiet repose I have ciphered the game,
That never on earth with this frail fleshly frame
Shall my heart lie content — though in lush valleys green —
No, only in death will my soul wax serene …

And only when heavenly angels lift up
This son of immortals, with joy I shall sup
Of ageless wine plentifully held in this cup …
The fruit of life perfectly lived will erupt,

In spiritual passions unfurled when I see
No more need I worry 'bout flesh's fickle decree;
Release from pain of error … imperfection …
To glorious lights of crystal sea's reflection.

Guatemala. *As a little child free of the cares of this world, rejoicing each day in discovering new and magnificent truths about the creation all around us, so is the one who has rejected the captivity of worldly idols and is determined to not allow rejection by others to rule over them.*

Chapter 4 Captivity, Freedom, Marginalization

Frivolity of Men

O men of vanity, children of the wind, born of desert places, corrupted by the heathen,
Words of frivolity bedeck your conscience, and living waters escape your abiding place.
The ways of life forsake your going out and coming in, shallow subjects and cackling laughter shielding your discomfort.
Eternal wisdom becomes lost amidst confusion of Babylon's merciless captivity,
Loss of righteous moorings, hopeless in irrationality consumed by human goods, unstable in virtue;
Dictated by princes set on high, rulers of men, your lives submitting, life's fruits wanting of soundness.
Rise up in goodness, dear creature of dust, and perceive your heritage,
your destiny as Israel …
If Israel you are ….

Now … and Tomorrow

Thrust suddenly upon the earth, a child in God's great Master Plan,
With time in His command, a truth so little understood — why now, not then? —
I sojourn in righteous indignation against the Adversary's hand,
Exposing his perverse, immoral attributes by the very substance of my life;
No place to lay this weary head upon earth's spoiled face — aching for release from bondage to corruption —
And I, its child of time's provision, search valiantly for that road to peace
Never to be found within this thraldom to decay, this failed, broken image of the heavenly.
Thus my search is doomed should earth's tainted grandeur be my quest …

Continued on page 39

Captivity, Freedom, Marginalization

Continued from page 38

But that brilliantly lit road to peace leads nowhere amongst the broken wrecks
of terra firma,
Only to that heavenly Zion which no flesh may yet see, no clay can this day perceive.
So I peer upward toward that hope wherein all men must hope,
To the never-ending joy of God's realm, that beginning and end of all existence,
The resting place of men made in His image, the place from which he came,
In Christ's footsteps, in the perfect way of the Pioneer of our salvation,
To the magnificent end of this earthly sojourn, to the very throne of all power and love …
To kingship and honor and glory and joy unending,
To fulfilling the utter purpose for which men were made to BE …
The I AM — self-existent, perfected ones — never again to sin, never again to fail,
But forever exulting within the ageless bosom of the Father' realm,
Where in all power and peace and love I may reach out and lift up my brothers unimpeded,
And create worlds within that glorious plan
That shall in due time be revealed to me and to those called …
Who can never be a part of this world's perverse dreams,
Its wayward, corrupt heart and lost and lonely schemes,

But thrust upon earth's sallow face
They run the race in love's pursuit,
Imbued through never-ending faith
That soon this pain would bear its fruit.

Chapter 4

Captivity, Freedom, Marginalization

Once a Captive

I was a captive in a foreign land …

My spirit searching for freedom from city's grip — concrete and steel, traffic and restless crowds, factories and prison-like schools surrounding me,
Unbending and heartless, confused in purpose, lost to steamy self-concerns, inward passions.

I was a prisoner in an alien place …

The forests green, lush, and inviting, but pierced by vicious bears preying on elk, and falcons and hawks slaying hapless hares and mice,
Expansive prairies glorious with pasqueflowers and bluestem, then charred by raging wildfires and summer's hail and wind.

I was a captive in a strange country …

Neighbors friendly and kind, but paying homage to idols of their own making, of autos, lands, homes, gold, and stone,
Countrymen lending money with usury, enslaving colleagues with debt unending, capturing widows and orphans to bondage and sweat shops.

I was a lost soul in a forbidden region …

Fed by fiery behemoths plying once-rich soils, with tools that bite and devour the elements of life, feeding markets of soulless traders,
Whose maws can never be filled, whose avarice cannot be quenched, and whose merchandising plies earth and sea.

Continued on page 41

But now I am free …

Free to roam the prairies and forests of my Edenic visions, far from predation and violence, for I know they are real.
Unleashed to flee the city's grip, to build a glorious homeland of my own that hustling trucks and trains, airports and belching industry cannot touch.
Liberated from the lure of idols and the captivity of debt to men, granting love and compassion to the needful, true bread to the hopeless.
Released from the iron bit of the plow, and the ships that seize the soil's gifts of wealth and trade them to countries far at sea.

Free, at liberty, purchased from bondage,
Restored to the one whom I truly was meant to be,
By the One who lives within me and has given new life,
A new heaven and a new earth.

We, the Initiated

We care not for the sound of earthly chimes nor the din of city's climes, or engine's ghastly whines,
But rest secure in wind's gentle sigh, through trees glistening neigh, beneath blue, cloud-studded sky.
We, the initiated …
We, the seers of things not seen by neighbors and friends …
We, the outcasts of hill and valley, prairie and forest,
Unable to cast aside the dream engraved within our minds,
That Eden shall return to earth's sallow, aging face,
And once again joy might possess the souls of men,
Their families and their lands cast free from bondage.

Chapter 5 Cities

City's Demise

Oh, evil city,
How you tread underfoot the hopes and dreams of the righteous …
  the poor … the needy in tears.
How your concrete footpaths point weary souls to Gehenna,
  and sap the vitals of the lost and maimed.
Your hot breath steams endlessly from London's infernal entrails,
Churning corruption from ill-gotten gain of the masses … the hungry,
  the lost.
May your posterity see light.
May your creator be banished at age's end.

Desperate People

Desperate people, crying for love,
Searching discretely for strength from above;
Seeking the high road but finding the low,
While struggling blindly amid mankind's flow.

Striving along as the bitter cold shakes
With utter abandon the clear crystal flakes
Of sense and discretion, those long-lost kind words,
Thrown off from dispassionate urbanite herds.

Egypt. *Cities around the world have an uncanny similarity in that people are crowded into a small area as so many rats in cages, apart from the natural world. Only the level of technology differs from place to place.*

Chapter 5 Cities

Hong Kong

Hong Kong steaming, seething with passion, confusion,
Mired in blackness of night at noonday, thrashing about aimlessly,
City of five million survivors with tear-filled faces,
Doting upon Babylon's fame, famished of truth, fluent in pride,
Gathered beneath an aura of perplexity, overshadowing branches
Of grotesque deformity from Eden's gardens, Zion's lofty heights,
Sister of merchants far and wide across earth's sighing face,
Readied for the great fall of end time's grand upheaval,
Concrete and steel falling amidst heaving ocean waves
Cleansing finally man's loathsome sore, festering feverishness,
While lost souls grope for hope — knowing not which hand to hold.

Impressions of the City

A muffled, distant roar 'neath leaden skies,
Dark snowflakes sifting down upon disgrace,
Night's acrid, pungent, frozen breeze to face,
While lovers stroll 'mid heartbreak, pure despise,
Of worlds so lost the eye must calmly bear
Such breach of nature's laws where squirrels now chase
Some crumbs from neighbor's refuse free from care.

Long streets, skyscrapers rising high above,
Sprawling suburbs crush lost cries for love
From homes of slaves who face the coming night
With horror, "Look, tomorrow's work we spite!"
Bright headlights stifle quests of why we're here;
Steel beasts entrap me, gears and fears so near.

Yet one lonely bird sings softly into the night.

New York City. *Manhattan Island creates a formidable view from the air, the heartbeat of worldwide finances and residence of thousands jammed into a very small area, so much so that streets resemble canyons where little direct sunlight reaches street level.*

Cities

Lament Over Melbourne

My heart hangs heavily against the din amongst skyscrapers, concrete,
and steel of mankind's imagination,
Intelligence misapplied through society's evil bent, love of money,
quest for greatness in eyes of other men,
Painful hearts uneasy, restless, sighing while roaming sidewalks faceless
alongside rushing humanity,
Babylon renewed, races white, yellow, black, and between rushing towards goals
unexamined, unrequested,
Planted firmly in place by generations of wayfarers equally lost,
Degeneration compounded through years of suffering abject poverty of spirit.
Melbourne's steely clouds lay hard upon the tiny ants scurrying below,
And I suffer the pain of lost hope in mankind's redemption.
Lost to himself, lost to his Maker, he struggles in quest for purpose,
Sensing his poverty but knowing no remedy of reprieve or repair.
In patience I shall await the clearing of the stratus over city and spirit,
For above the overcast shines bright light — the sun in full strength.
My heart shall never waver from seeking bright heaven's starry vision,
For there lies my home, in the Father's eternal realm.

Italy. *Though ancient cities of Europe possess a somewhat different flavor than the modern centers of commerce in many New World countries, they still build house to house and leave little room for the natural world to find a place in their midst.*

Cities

London Streets

Lonely strangers walk "clip-clop" down concrete sidewalks,
Along treeless boulevards, beside bare buildings of stone,
Faceless, ignoring all others … even themselves …
As winter's cold bears in and loveless hearts exalt themselves,
Refusing to look up from cold concrete and let in love,
Preying upon neighbors, enlarging adulteries, lusting after mammon,
A generation inviting painful reproof through heinous sins,
Knowing not the source of light that would save them.

Moscow in Spring

Moscow in spring, faceless, helpless slaves of monotony, morose
and unsmiling
But for a few.
Children ever hopeful, mothers and grandfathers hand-in-hand with joy,
Survival plotting courses of love amidst suppressed hysteria of
countless bustling Russians
Intent on staying the course, surviving the holocaust,
Not knowing why this agony, these smoggy, eye-biting, murky streets,
The white, hard bread stacked in neat piles which never satisfies,
The din of engines and dangerous streets: why?
Moscow groans and trembles, shivers and shakes at her fate.

Continued on page 50

Chile. *The cities of South America differ little from those of North America, possessing skyscrapers in the business district that seem to satisfy the pride of business people who work within such towers of Babel.*

Chapter 5

Cities

Continued from page 48

Modern czars holding fates of uncounted millions in bloody hands,
Medes and Persians, Khazars and Mongols, Georgians and
Israelites all poised
To flee the sword should chaos again afflict Tubal and Meshech,
To cower in fear once again amongst dingy gray streets and
concrete walls of slavery.

New York JFK Airport

Rancor, confusion, bustle, folly
Hustling along halls of latter day civilization,
Lumped into a seething sea of humanity tied together by the most
delicate threads,
Flesh striving with flesh, greed meeting vanity;
Mothers with children untaught and wild — dark children, light children,
Junkies, the hopeless, the arrogant, foreigners,
Despondent souls, exhausted savants, studious scholars,
All tossed into one basket, thoroughly mixed;

Impatient ticket checkers, sorting some order from the chaos,
Tired, stressed clerks and checkers at metal detectors,
Highly painted faces of ladies masquerading beauty …
Yet compounding garishness with tight-fitting dresses.

Continued on page 53

Colombia. *The prolific graffiti found in many cities typifies the desire of many impromptu artists to somehow cover over the steel and concrete monotony of building upon building, and introduce a semblance of life amongst the lifelessness.*

KR 2ª
CARRERA 2A
16A-04

Continued from page 50

I think one thought — to get out, to stay out,
Out of this cacophony of frightened and confused flesh,
This depository of fear and vanity pawned off as indispensable
To a lost world struggling for sanity.

One World

Every city the same, each venue a clone of the next —
Des Moines, Dallas, Miami, Bangkok, Santiago, Capetown, Brussels, Rome, Cairo, Moscow, Delhi —
Restless people in God's image hurrying, worrying, wondering
What the day might thrust upon them,
Striving to survive, not knowing why, just being who they are,
Yet not knowing the One who made them,
The great One who could show them the way, calm their fears,
Release from bondage the spirit captured to ignorance.
Bring an end, great God, to the facade of peace,
That the sameness of cities, and the wantonness of mankind,
May blossom forth into abundance for all races,
All peoples, all lost souls on earth!

Ghana. *Most cities, especially large ones, invariably contain ghettos and deprived areas where families subsist as best they can. Many inhabitants have no home at all, and live on sidewalks or underpasses, and some beg for handouts.*

Chapter 5 Cities

Sydney in the Morning

Lumbering silver bird, gliding upon rarified air into cool harbor's berth,
Daughter of Babylon's worldwide net, gaudy lights shimmering as
deceptive beacons towards cold Pacific waters,
Ships plying trader's wealth to distant shores,
Godlessness, hedonism, materialism, worship of men's creations her fare,
As for all cities of Babylon's clutch,
Her heart cold, forsaking love, glorifying mindless selfish gain,
For what? She does not ask …

What life is —
What the Master's plan is —
Why man?

Sydney — ignorant today, but hopeful yet
When tomorrow's sun rises upon wisdom and true knowledge,
Wiping away today's darkness that soon must pass.

Restless City

The restless city never stops, never rests,
Beating coldly upon its tarnished pavement,
Breathing fire from its frothing nostrils …
Besmirching the earth with its tirade of futile existence
For reasons it cannot articulate …
Except in cold, hard roarings of motors and perplexed people,
Caught up in themes and schemes they cannot fathom.

Australia. *Even in far-off Australia the urge to build city centers upwards is evident, people preferring to concentrate themselves in urban centers and evacuate the surrounding countryside, at least for the day. Then so many flee to natural areas on weekends and vacations to try and regain sanity among the trees and lakes, the greens and blues of the creation.*

Cities

The City At Night

The clock nears midnight, its "tick-tick" hastening on into the night,
And the city lays brightly, pompously against the blackened sky,
Gleaming out harshly into space, its breath hot and heavy,
its heartbeat ceaselessly pounding.

"Tick-tick", the pendulum swings.
Oh, savor the soul whose destiny brings
Him out of the shadow to broad light of day,
Redounding in hope lest his own heart should say:

"You, my offspring, are mine."
No, never shall such be mine!

Cast off the cords which bind and blind,
And shatter the bosom of whoredom's own kind,
Her nakedness luring each soul to its net
Of unabashed carnal unskirted lament.

And passions rush in fever strength
Toward twisted orphans' hell-bent stink.

"Prefer the light of day, my hope,
Though trains and trucks through darkness grope,"
She said with gleaming, sin-filled eye,
Without a tear to shed or cry:

For those trampled down;
Hopes thrust rudely to the ground.

Brazil. *The large cities of Brazil are no exception to the sameness found in metropolitan areas across the world, accommodations oftentimes moving upwards to increase the concentration of humans even more.*

Chapter 5

Cities

The Subway in London

Smoggy, acrid wind through steel and stone canyoned chasms,
Dashing hulks of steel moaning, roaring insanely,
As worried crowds in swaying coats descend — down, down, into dirty dungeons —
Down squealing escalators — or stalled ones — ever further into Hades.
Grimy walls, tracks, train cars rock along the depths of London,
Through caverns lit like daytime, hurried Englishmen, blacks, yellows,
Squeezed within hollow metal cocoons, uneasy, silent, afraid to see and be seen,
Rocking gently through darkness and bright station-stops,
Hoards of lost souls grasping for solace,
Servants of the world lost in time,
Seeing evil but knowing not its reformation.

The City

City lights glowing ominously from distant horizons,
Challenging twinkling starlight with coarse, unnerving glow,
Cast dim shadows through darkened skies, car lights trailing sinister roars on distant highways,
Echoes of city's civilization beckoning death to freedom, wisdom, and hope.

The Wind and the City

Oh restless winds of winter's night, your voice has cried so long,
Above the din of traffic's flight and airport's rumbling song.
Among the lights in drawn-out beads, tall structures bar your path,
As fog horns blare and engines speed, shrill sirens speed and dash.

Continued on page 59

Continued from page 58

You've visited this land so long, its wooded shores recall,
When but a lonely Indian throng with care delayed its fall;
Not knowing soon the land would cry, its life-blood sorely spent,
The sweet, serene, and azure sky befouled through man's descent.

Your journeys long have viewed this scene as care seemed like a pawn,
As man's slow mind and blinded scheme moved beauty, joy, bright song
Behind its towering treasures tall where grasping gentile hands
Seem deathly bent on their own fall, and that of all their lands.

Where comes your patience, mighty wind, your power never ends.
In one quick stroke of gracious force to earth this plan you'd send,
If not for your own secret dream whose story great will live
Within an earth so tired of schemes ignorantly man gives.

Washington, Oh Washington

Rock and concrete edifices, stone-by-stone,
Cold, resolute, stolid against winter's February sun,
Dirt-mingled snow patchy on sidewalks,
Walls of repression stretching high above streets and sidewalks;
Over the Potomac, past the Washington Monument,
By the Lincoln Memorial, the White House,
Bureau of the Interior, State Department, Pentagon …
A nation sowing order amidst disorder,
Performing with difficulty;
A nation — all nations — in disarray, lacking knowledge,
Without proper wisdom, judgment, mercy,
Forsaking the widow and orphan, the cry of the humble,
Fattening coffers for self,
Annihilating bastions of truth, refusing to purchase wisdom.
In wide-eyed abandonment elected officials parade in order
Down marble corridors, oblivious of their destiny,
Forsaking the mandate of their Creator.
A mongrel people troop down gray concrete,
Victims of time's placement, seeking what pleasure may grant,
While life somehow clings within walled cities of repression.
Not a bird sings, not a face smiles; all is vanity,
As Washington, D.C., capital of the world's greatest power — Israel —
Hustles among the gentiles into oblivion.

Chapter 5 Cities

The City Asleep On Sunday Morning

The city asleep on Sunday morning.

Quiet against early August's deep blue vistas, dewy and fragrant sweetclover,
Planes and trains and trucks more silent, more subdued;
The vireos and goldfinches, crickets and thrushes more bold,
Heard above the former din of the haughty, hot furnace …

Of concealed hate,
Of unabashed carnality,
Of greedy eyes in search of more,
Of blank stares on scummed pavement.

The city asleep while morning tick-tocks the brutal peace away,

The sleep of death, of superstition,
Questions untold, minds as sheep shyly, placidly unaware
That the morning's peace is but a facade,
The truth lying elsewhere, hidden, for more sober minds …

As heads ache and hung over bodies roll over again,
Recalling the emptiness of yesterday's exploits,
Resolving to uncover new, moral vistas today …
But falling flatly as morning's sleep reclaims its victory once again.

The city asleep as church bells chime,

In voices melodic through the awesomely beautiful morning,
Greeting the sun, great god of this inglorious stupor,

Continued on page 61

Continued from page 60

While certain ones flock through doors of towered buildings
In search of peace the city cannot give,

For her sealed mission hidden from most,
From her master architect … of hate and disrespect …
Retains the warped structure of things beyond the grasp
Of hungry hands seeking the right way… but still lost.

The city asleep while faint breezes stir cottonwood leaves,

Wafting traces of earth, summer flowers, fresh cool morning air
Through the corner window,
Open to an empty plain where once stood farmsteads and families,
Herds and homes, happiness …

And I cry.
My head cannot rise, my mind is in pain,
For the countryside as well has fallen to the cruel master,
The architect of the lost sheep's abode this morning.

The city asleep,

While heavens quake,
As nations tool for war
And millions cry out in hunger,
Unable to quench the pangs that return each day … again, and again ….

Thus tears cannot quench the fire
This ugly monster has burning within the lives of the throngs.
Yet, another age at another time, when sleep has passed, when hope again rises strongly
Will wipe the tears away, gently, when the heated city is gone, utterly gone, and the sleep of Sunday morning is lost for eternity, a dim, sordid memory against the brilliant thrill of a new world.

Chapter 6

Countries

Leaders Without Leaders

They all rule tempestuously, these children of wrath,
Given to laudable goals but reserving the victory for abuse.
They have recalled but vanity, and go down to the dust,
Trusting in fortunes and fame, but forgetting from whence they came.

A Warning to the Nations

Oh, nation reprobate, mother of harlotry,
Bring to heel your evil sons and daughters.
Let not the end of your ways lead to the grave,
So be wary of your lawless days.
Change them to sunshine and rainbows,
And let in the light of the Eternal's mighty spirit,
Lest the sun set on your power.

Greenland Renewed

Rocky peaks protrude as lonely sentinels from Greenland's barren ice,
Racing by far beneath this great silver bird,
An inhospitable land once peopled abundantly,
As all earth once was teeming;
Indeed all land was meant to be fruitful and populated.
The desert and frozen lands cry out to man to turn from sin
So once again summer may burn away the ice and snow,
Rains may revive the barren, hot wastelands,
That all the earth might blossom and bear fruit.

China.

Human governments invariably place a person at the top of the rulership pyramid, in particular within a dictatorship where the leader is oftentimes considered to be next to god. Whether considered deified or not, these leaders so often run roughshod over the citizens and rule through fear and force.

Russia. *The glorification of human leaders knows no bounds, even within countries where the supreme ruler is brutal beyond imagination, slaughtering multiple millions and imprisoning even more in order to cast fear into the populace so they may remain in power.*

Russia Sighing

Sighing in slow death she lies beaten down,
Mother Russia — slave of Satan's dictators, pyramids of human power —
Men tired and confused, knowing good,
Yet unable to perform it, bureaucracies tying men's hands …
And to be safe the wise sit serenely, learning great patience,
Or wait lethargically on park benches, growing gaunt with want
From cupboards bare while families lay under siege
So lands and farms may not grow up in abundant fruitfulness.
They wallow helplessly in suppressed dormancy.
Greed of leaders' heavy hands bows the backs of governed millions
Intent on hope's fruition, but learning life's brutal lesson
That confronting the brutal Khazar race within Russia's bounds
Brings risks and brutality untold: "Not worth it", they say
And lie down, dejected again, reaching for Vodka to drown their sorrows.

Mother Russia

Sighing slow death lies beaten down,
Mother Russia — dictator's slave, shouldering brutal pyramids of power —
Tired men, pensive women … children too young to know …
Knowing good but hands neatly tied,
Safe in blind, painful serenity, fearful of the heavy hand,
Lethargy filling the cup — the nation grows gaunt.
Cupboards bare, families under siege,
Lands and cities suppressed … dormant;
Leaders' hardness crushes untold millions of dreams
In brutality, life's lost visions seeking relief.
Oh, for one ray of hope the millions gaze skyward,
Into a sky of blue and brilliance so few can see.

Chapter 6

Countries

Guatemala Farmers

Farmers and hikers laying on the cool, mountain grass of Guatemala hills
 and valleys,
Retreating from the rigors of hoeing for a respite;
Women in colorful dresses — faces golden brown and determined,
 Indian — washing clothes on rocks in rivers and ponds;
Quick showers that dampen children and women, pots on heads,
 hurrying along dirt paths between tall walls of corn;
Walking, walking, walking people, homes hanging against hillsides,
Fields impossible on hills too steep to walk …
A country of meditating shy girls and young ladies, wrinkled old men and women,
Time standing still,
Hopes and dreams mingled with mud brick, dirt-floored homes, rosy and
 smudged children,
Spartan lives … biggest tools a mattock … no more …
No need,
No need.

Delano, California. *The Statue of Liberty symbolizes the freedoms that Americans enjoy as outlined in the Constitution, such as freedom of speech, freedom to assemble at will, freedom of the press, and freedom to worship as one wills. As God-given as there rights might be, whole nations have lost them through reprobate behavior that led them into slavery, such as Israel when the nation rejected the commands of the Creator.*

CLAAS
LEXION
CLAAS
DANGER

Demise and Renewal of the Land

Sleep, O Pioneers

She decays, our mother countryside,
And in her wake rests the bones of her demise.

May our forefathers never awake to view this tragedy …
For horror and tears would fill their eyes.

Demise of the Farm

Rotting hulks of yesteryear's former glory and grandeur,
Once stately upon the Plain, once beacons of hope in mankind's tenure upon soils black as midnight.
Families thriving in hope, sweat, joy, frustration … but endless faith
That someday indeed this earth would yield its hidden wealth,
Rich Chernozem would release its treasured measure …
And bless fathers, mothers, sons, daughters, friends, and kin
With lasting peace and possession, rewards for man's labors, winning of the proud, solemn prairie.
I am with you, lost fathers, mothers, and children — turned to dust beneath the ceaseless, fretting prairie winds.
I am your son, hearty pioneer of fertile hope, sprouting vigorously from black earth.
I shall ever be your advocate, from now to eternity —
Lover of creation, defender of its eloquence, teaching Truth amidst the haughty perversity of your vacant, rotting hulks.
Lost dreams have visited you beyond measure
While you labored heroically under the blazing summer sun,
Breaking the sod, seeding wheat upon virgin soil, waiting upon tender sprouts to thrust upwards their vigorous heads …

Continued on page 70

Chapter 7

Demise and Renewal of the Land

Continued from page 69

Then harvesting the golden fields, first by scythe and then by reaper,
Threshing the hearty bread of life for you and your brethren to live …
Ah yes, to LIVE on this fair earth, and reap her bounteous rewards.
I am your son and your brother;
I am your kinsman and protector.
I am with your spirit in the grave,
A watchman over your vision of men and families at peace upon the land,
Beneath their own vine and fig tree,
Free of distress and the portent of disaster soon to strike …
Like you were struck in quiet devastation upon the fertile plain
That never intended to eject you, never designed you to walk away
from this fortune of wealth.
You are gone, gone and lost by Satan's wiles and whims,
The archenemy having given your grain to the enemy,
Lifted the alien on high,
And taught your brothers perversion and lawlessness.
Even your hardiest souls have fallen prey to the siren song of fleshpots
and the all-seeing eye.
Your land is corrupted without remedy, led to utter desolation by
the evil shepherds
Whose insanity has swept up with a bitter vortex all but the elect into
her dying, crying, burning midst.
I cry over the beautiful vision these rotting hulks have left behind,
Of hopes unhidden by their builders, of dreams without limit …
But squandered just when victory was in sight,

Continued on page 73

Sinai, South Dakota. *The iron bite of the mouldboard plow has caused a great amount of soil erosion over the decades since the prairies and forests of America were first broken and farmed. This loss of soil fertility — the strength of the nation — continues today in spite of the fact that minimum tillage has increased over the past years.*

California. *Millions of acres of land in many countries have been converted to salty, unfarmable wastelands due to irrigation with salty water and intensive farming practices. The abrogation of natural laws in crop management, in particular tillage, continues to destroy the integrity of farmland throughout the world.*

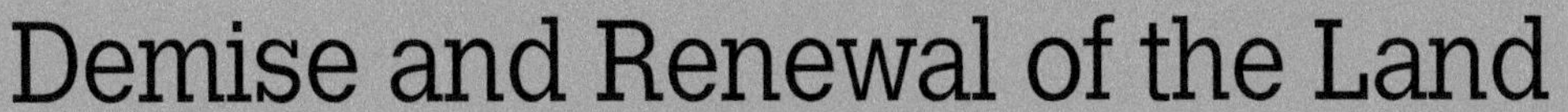

Demise and Renewal of the Land

Continued from page 70

When the wages of the laborers were deftly withheld and cast away in thievery
To a brutal cast of players,
An unholy crowd of hades' design.
Renew Your plan, great God.
Design again the earth and mankind on it in brilliant joy.
Once again let families thrive in peace, joy, and hope fulfilled upon a fruited plain
For a millennium of years.
You have promised it; You will cause it be.
Bring us Your hope fulfilled once again, great God,
And forget not Your servants who constantly plead for Your return.

Farm to Cities, Dust to Dust

The land languishes, cringes under stout, brutal hands of exploiters,
spoilers of resources,
Cold machines of steel racing across hills and valleys, rupturing earth's skin,
exposing sores across the Plain …
And pelting thunderstorms roar unmercifully upon the barren soil,
roiling her unprotected wealth seaward
As sons of men steam out their lives upon the land, struggling to survive through
debt-driven poverty,
Assessed against priceless resources, future's hope … cast upon destroying winds and rains.
Young men stream to colleges of false values, idle pursuit, technology gone amuck,
Seldom to return to fertile fields and pastures of their youth — now bereft of
morning's invigorating ozone,
Or the day's sweat and toil in priceless pursuit of true wealth … and sweet sleep
at day's end.
Farm to city, dust to dust, prosperity to poverty, all is quiet
As a nation forsakes its roots in the heavenly and grovels in the fleshpots of the earthly.

Demise and Renewal of the Land

If This Old Farmhouse Could Speak

South winds sweep across rolling plains of corn, beans, and wheat.
Still, gray house, last paint flaking, shingles shoddy and split,
Grass matted and unkempt, windbreak trees tall and full —
  stark contrast — in last-stand defiance,
Yet some dead or dying, giving up the fight.

  I ask, "What say you, gray house of my prairie fathers,
  Lying dying against the awesome powers of wind,
    thunderstorm, blizzard, and baking heat?
  What say you, within your vacant rooms gathering dust,
  Window shades askew, door frames naked and unpainted?
  What stories do you tell of your master's life, his hopes and dreams,
  His wife, children laughing and playing before the wintertime wood stove,
  Loyal neighbors' firm knock on the door, oxen teams jingling gear
    in nearby fields.
  What say you now, fallen relic of bygone years?
  Why do you brood so pensively, staring eastward at the rising sun,
  Her dancing rays playing mirror games with waving box elder boughs
  And lilac twigs upon those windows yet unbroken?"

So silently the house lies unspeaking, still denying death's relentless
  spirit creeping in
Upon this farmland vanquished through the forces thrust upon her …
Aliens upon the land, subtly sapping fertile grains and forage
From the rich black gold laid bare by plow, disk, and steel-toothed weapons.

Continued on page 77

Porter, Minnesota.

Prairie farmsteads at one time served as the headquarters of thriving farm communities, until the great move from animal to tractor power enabled farmland to consolidate into larger spreads, driving many farmers off the land. These old structures are becoming fewer and fewer as the deteriorating houses and barns are torn down and bulldozed into oblivion.

Demise and Renewal of the Land

Continued from page 74

Sod house was your mother, the choicest of Norway's pioneers your father.
They built you strong to stand against the wind and hail.
Powerfully you stood, white as snow while yet the nation preached of goodness,
kindness, faith, and peace …
But dim corruption entered heaven's gates,
And thrust down peaceful enclaves you designed to keep.

Alas the gauntlet fell, and pride overtook the fruited plain, the budding forest, the
vaunted city,
And alien forces rose up strong — the slave from the pit, the Edomite from the Pale —
To rape the wealth your master so meticulously reaped day and night
From field, flock, and forest … fruits of blessed rains and summer's tempestuous winds.

The farms grew large, the wages small; your neighbors sighed through stresses flung
Upon the choicest men on earth: no love of money threw them off the plain,
But relentless forces tearing at the roots of a race first given wealth of soil, flock,
Blessings of fields, cities, rivers, and gold.

Then too the family of this house abandoned hopes of future realms
Of Jacob's seed laughing, playing, racing joyfully around the white walls,
Within the small but well-kept rooms
Of one small kingdom set amongst so many millions,
Once thriving, now deposed amidst fiat money's fickle promise …
Invention of the serpent breed sown subtly among the wheat and barley,
Released as Pandora's box was opened, just a crack, yet a crack too wide.

Continued on page 78

New Zealand. *The grower of grapes is prophesied to reap untold bounty within a renewed environment when the new Eden arrives. The extent of increased production will be incredible, beyond our wildest dreams.*

Demise and Renewal of the Land

Continued from page 77

Now fruits of industry, seeds of despair from geneticists' misguided minds,
Chemicals of death, machines to further tear and crush soil's life,
Surround this still, gray house.
If only these weathered boards, these darkened abandoned rooms could speak
The songs of hope denied, the memories of children laughing, rejoicing,
Of farmers and wives toiling, hands blackened by soil and grease,
Furrows of worry creasing their brows and cheeks.

But through the wrinkles lay the hopes of worlds renewed,
Even as the family loaded its last chair, teddy bear, and kitchen cup,
And turned to glimpse the bright white house against the backdrop of fall's sullen,
stratus-covered sky …
Tears gleaming in saddened eyes
As the loaded truck crept down the gravel driveway to the township road,
Never to return, no, never again.

If this old farmhouse could speak it would not fail to bid you comfort.
The roof will leak, timbers will rot, and in due season a farmer will bring it down.
When that shall happen, and fuel dries up, the weeds return to triumph over the spray,
And man waxes weak from crops so bereft of strength that farmers hardly care to wake,

Then this land shall enjoy her Sabbaths,
And sky will turn cold and ashen;
The sun will not give her light, nor the moon her strength …
And all of creation in great anticipation
Will await the return of its King of Kings,
And this old house — and its bulldozed foundation lying beneath this rich, black earth —
Will regain her strength,
Never again to be removed from Jacob's blessed inheritance.

Michigan. *Fruit crops such as cherries will thrive throughout the new Eden on earth, but not just cherries; an array of crops perhaps never before experienced will be brought into production, growing freely throughout the landscape for anyone to eat and enjoy.*

Chapter 7

Demise and Renewal of the Land

Lost Valley of Youth

Once you were a beauty, my love,
Bubbling, living waters meandering in laughter between grassy, mossy banks
Through valleys broad and fertile, bluestem shoulder high beyond the aged, giant pecans,
willows, and cottonwoods that hugged your banks,
Cool, damp, southerly breezes beneath steel-gray skies beckoning rain to again
wet your soul with life.
You were young then, young and supple, gorgeous in your array of fall leaves bedecking
each nook and cranny along your banks,
Little dams of leaves shrouding minnows and trout, content beneath icy water.
Shimmering, beautiful you were in your prime, deer and bison, lynx and bear your companions.

But today, my love, you have fallen … not through willful neglect or perverted desire;
Your master has forsaken you, plowing and grazing your watershed until waters rushed
from summer's rain,
Roiling your laughing waters into harsh roaring, boiling torrents of brown and dirty gray.
Rushing currents tore asunder your enclosing banks, leaving cliffs of blackened decay,
roots helplessly clinging to barren earth.
But alas, flood after flood tore at your bed, raping your helpless virginity,
Leaving summer's still water hot and murky, dead and lifeless, stinky and sudsy.
Lumberjacks harvested the choicest giant trees along your banks; cattle grazed grass
to bare soil year after year, sparing nothing …
Showing no remorse for your shores and valleys, your former beauty and joy.
Now you lay barren and naked, patriarchs lying dead and dying along your course,
though fall's wonder of golden leaves yet wave above in winds less pure,
Winds often bitter and harsh, storms unforgiving and destructive.

I pine in despair, my love.
I cry in utter grief at your loss, your depravity,
A wife forsaken by an unthinking husbandmen,

Continued on page 81

Demise and Renewal of the Land

Continued from page 80

Even a virgin cast out because of her goodness, purity, and excellence
That her keeper could not bear to view amidst his own evil exploits.

My hope lies in tomorrow, my love.
Your Maker shall clean you up, renew you to an even lovelier visage than before.
No longer shall you lie in naked disgust before my pain-stricken eyes.
Each day your bubbling water shall greet countless caring husbandmen
Loving you, loving each other,
Loving life instead of heartache …
For you shall be beauty, hope, joy, and purity for all the earth.
You shall drip renewal as honey amidst the fruitful hills,
And faith as ruler over all the Kingdom.

Lost Way On the Land

A bright, sunny week's first day, and all is quiet but for warblers, doves, crows, and geese,
A clear blue canopy shining upon verdant trees and grasses of yesterday's passions,
Settlers conquering prairie's rich treasures, breaking sod, sowing wheat and corn,
    harvesting golden treasures
From earth black as midnight, fertile beyond compare, terra firma's richest blessings;
Families large and strong, hearty of soul, supple of mind and body,
Ready, able to conquer and subdue, exercise dominion, tame a land preserved for centuries …

Just for them,
Just for them.

Then a plague assaulted their midst, a horrible, wrenching curse,
Beyond drought, hailstorms, locusts, and disease …

Continued on page 83

Michigan. *Berry crops will abound throughout the earth on a greatly increased land area in the new age, and being perennials they will require only minor tending and keeping, as Adam and Eve experienced in the Garden of Eden.*

Demise and Renewal of the Land

Continued from page 81

A sickness of poverty, the masters of exchange withholding just rewards for labor,
Through stealth of money — love of its twisted worth — milking the land through furrowed, sweaty brows
Of laboring fathers and worried mothers, sheltering children from Babylon's oncoming scourges as best they could.
Now Israel's land lies quiet and humbled, buried in debt,
Pheasants crowing in distant fencerows, joyful cries of children no longer heard amongst the decaying walls and collapsing roofs
Of barns, houses, and sheds, their testimony of abandonment shouting to every passerby … but not heard, not perceived
By unseeing eyes and media-seared hearts.
Yet, the flies, cicadas, and mosquitoes buzz and hum as they always have.
The grass and thistles still secure the rich soil of abandoned farmsteads,
Monarch, painted lady, yellow sulfur, and swallowtail butterflies yet flutter deftly across flower-bespeckled, unmowed farmyards …
And I cry huge tears of sadness for the families long-since displaced to a foreign land,
The seeds of their destruction sown in sin and rebellion to the Most High.
Yet, I still lament this quiet debacle of year-by-year, decade-by-decade desolation of the land.
Far from this legacy grew Israel's roots, a mighty, glowing heritage
Of true wealth and happiness,
The land of fertile prosperity, of a marvelous way of life — the backbone of society's strength —
Now sown to business and money, forces of politics and global wealth.
The families are gone, and last vestiges of families sit hoping for relief …
For recovery that shall come at the end of days,
When a new Eden shall fill this land with song!

Demise and Renewal of the Land

Renewal On the Prairie

Wooden edifice of cultures past lay dying, rotting,
Old shingles tattered and soft, rain dripping through breaches
In a roof long unattended, wind vanes askew, doors gone,
Window frames shattered, boards orange with lichens,
Windmill without rotors, mere steel jutting skyward;
A chicken house nearly flattened nearby, one last wall about to topple,
One nest amidst the rubble yet reminding of its past utility,
Now cast away amidst futility.
A gray, open-windowed house peeks silently through shrouding trees,
Hidden along with countless struggles and dreams of lost pioneers.
As carcasses of men's dreams decay and sink into the earth.
Beautiful trees and shrubs spring up alongside their embarrassed hulks,
Elms, cottonwoods, basswoods, box elders, and ash reaching for the sun,
Overreaching, overshadowing the rotting death of failed quests lost in time.
Winds gently sway the boughs, the honeysuckle, and bromegrass carpet.
Sunshine plays upon the moist, supple greenery, casting glints through
newly fallen raindrops.
All of creation relentlessly, irresistibly covers this tragedy, erasing the pain,
This alarming travesty yet playing out its silent debacle upon the prairie's tired face.
What remains and is built of life is what was meant to be.
Glorious shades of green are victorious over dying, crumbling browns and grays
Of yesteryear's failed schemes, wrought in ignorance,

Continued on page 86

New Zealand. *Untold production of all crops will be the norm once the present age has passed, and the atmospheric gases, sunlight, moisture conditions, and temperatures will be optimized — as they were in Eden — and plant pests and economic upheavals will no longer inhibit prosperity and abundance.*

Chapter 7 Demise and Renewal of the Land

Continued from page 85

Fought without knowledge, lost when wealth-hungry magnates
Demanded the blood of the land to serve their insatiable, abominable thirst
For power and dominion over men set in array at the base of all wealth …
Tillers of fields and shepherds of flocks — foundation builders —
Cut down and cast into hasty graves as so much dross,
Though rains fell wonderfully and crops grew tall and proud.
So little the marketers of thievery gave, and dreams died.
To cities the children fled, and tillers and shepherds lived out their years,
While the decaying evidence of former habitats bore stark testimony
To all the world of the terrible error fraught here,
But also of joyous days ahead,
When Trees of Life will spring up mightily and overshadow
The rusting, rotting hulks of the prairie's lost dreams,
And cast in permanence new-found hope upon their land …
When barns, homes, and windmills shall not fail,
And smiles will grace the faces of little children
Born with the blood of eternity in their veins,
Never again to be moved from the land of promise.

Demise and Renewal of the Land

Chapter 7

The Prairie's Demise

Up rise the steel towers from the plain,
As house upon house the fields reveal their stain,

Larger and larger grow the farms, memories lost of past days,
When families grew and thrived along broad, supple ways.

"Bigger, bigger, better, better!" cry self-proclaimed merchants of conformity and law,
As mercy and love know not their abode amid coldness which seems never to thaw.

Down bow the heads to materialism and goods, to money and physical venture,
While men of golden stature find grief amid such perverted adventures.

"Arise, prefer the whims of uninstructed conscience, and fabricate personal law:"
So pontificate mindless men, mincing mighty proverbs to fall vainly beneath the jaw.

Realms of confused effeminates flock to doors of brothels,
minds steaming of perversities,
While never gratified, the mind wanders aimlessly over fields of perplexities.

Oh, release the grip of the heathen's aspirations upon this fertile ground,
And breath paradise's renewal to every creature, and call them back to Eden found.

Education, Computers, Humanism

A Trip to the Library

Verbiage, verbiage, profuse wordage,
Stalks the halls of frozen stirrage,

Grasping for the bits of peace,
Swimming through the grime and grease.

Subjects here, subjects there,
Paper, paper everywhere,

Bound into assorted muddle,
Glued together with much trouble.

Hairs grow grayer, heads a-swimming,
Muscles aching, eyes a-dimming,

Poring priceless pages frightful ...
Seeking pleasures more delightful.

Farson, Wyoming. *The fundamentals of present-day education have become more of an indoctrination into political correctness than a teaching of the three Rs, a course that is like traveling a road to nowhere, the end of which will bring heartache and regret.*

Chapter 8 Education, Computers, Humanism

Education

Lessons, lessons pound away through the dreary live-long day,
Facts remembered thick and heavy that in tests teachers may levy.
Year by year the mind takes in assorted details … what a sin
That somehow pointless points don't match, the fragmented mind a thatch
Of bits and pieces glued with paste unto the brain in breakneck haste.
Bind the will to earthly ways so in this life you'll spend you days
Building dreams for fathers' sakes … same old lessons, same mistakes
Stressed upon the holocaust … history's portents long since lost.
Then I asked with wrinkled hand, standing near the promised land,
What was learned 'midst four gray walls, mind-churn factories, lecture halls:
How to be a sadder man, how to live as humdrums can …
Creativity erased, Eden's hopeful quest effaced.
But as for me — oh, yes I cried — yet while my helpless classmates sighed
I saw the broad dark road ahead, where truth reigned dim, to mis'ry led,
Resolved to cast the dross aside, while holding wisdom close beside.

Pritchett, Texas. *Education for the younger generation was meant to begin with the examples and teachings of the older generation, to pass along the lessons of life that will safeguard these new inductees into life, making grandparents so incredibly valuable to civilization's progress and stability.*

Chapter 8

Education, Computers, Humanism

Language in Darkness

No language of men today can express
The joy of angels and sons of God,
The love of man for his Maker,
The peace he longs for to direct his steps.
He struggles to clear a way of wisdom,
Yet finds his way besmirched by meanings
Unattainable within the illogical symbols
Of words bequeathed by masters of millennia ago,
When Babylon lost her wits and nations scattered
To earth's four corners at the Eternal's bidding.

Thus earth groans on for lack of expression
With words and symbols replete with transgression.
Language of men, anchored to lines
All tangled in frustrating jumbles and twines,
Drifting in unfathomed, blind disarray,
Disabled expression through history's sway.

Elohim's language to Adam was taught,
Disrupted in chaos … dark angel's fought
To bury pure wisdom amidst troubled tongues
As Babylon stumbled on tower's weak rungs.

Then Persia descended on Babylon's heels,
And further perverted world's central appeals,
While family dispersion brought clustering curds …
A million translations of once perfect words.

Fond Grecian confused mindset further despaired
Of upright conversion for tongue's verbiage shared
By Rome's tattered legions of smoldering might …
Iron with clay, men despairing of light.

Continued on page 93

Education, Computers, Humanism

Chapter 8

Continued from page 92

Age upon age, brutal rape of pure tongue,
Down to the grave crude insanity flung
Man's age in chaos since wisdom was cursed,
When language no longer in spirit was versed.

Modern Life

Hectic, scatterbrained, divided, perverse,
Sterile, discomfiting, unhealthy, nerve-racking,
Noisy, crude, crass, hopeless,
Causeless, soft, difficult, dangerous,
Unrighteous, evil, ensnaring, carnal.

Computers stare red-eyed captives face-to-face,
Unfeeling, uncaring, unmoving, cold subjects of programs,
Dictating worlds of peril to masses of millions,
Complicating the simple,
Tearing joy from her moorings,
Creating programs and systems of multiplied complexities,
Unfathomable, infinitely intricate nature
Stomped underfoot
Without feeling, without care …
Guided by underworld powers remaking worlds
After destructions' evil name,
Seeking sameness in diversity's face,
Locking horns with entropy,
The assured victory of sanity and godliness ignored …
For this one fleeting moment across eternity's glistening, tear-filled face.

Chapter 8 Education, Computers, Humanism

Release from Humanism

Surrounded by green trees, leafy and vibrant … by angels unseen, quiet, powerful,
Soft Australian wind to my back, sun brilliant above, clouds few but pure and white,
Awesome day resting peacefully with my spirit, a sweet savor to the Creator,
Reserved so preciously
For souls truly blessed, specially granted the choicest portion of earth's smiling face,
Her greatest wonders shining forth messages of tender hope amidst the
hopelessness of billions lost,
Who seek solace but find none,
Restless and encumbered by humanism's prison.

Captive to Immodesty

Young ladies in bright outfits, revealing parts best hidden,
Sensual, purveying obvious loose living … this to be
The way portrayed as right, yet unbeknownst to them
A ploy for captivity, bondage stronger than steel,
For wealth of the rich, exploited bodies and dreams
In lucrative commerce to drain vitality of men and nations,
Enriching merchant's exploitation, marketing ladys' ignorance.

The iPad

Heads lie buried, captured by bits in little boxes,
Held by hands uncalloused, mesmerized by flickering screens,
Led into a land of fairy tales and mindless dreams,
Failing life's decisive battles, led down paths obnoxious.

Yellowstone Park, Wyoming. *The greatest education for young children—and certainly for oldsters as well— is to see up-close the creation that surrounds us when we venture into untamed lands. Humanism, cell phones, and the theory of evolution cannot stand when confronted with the realities that God has set before us, if we will but look, and allow true education to consume us.*

Russia. *The buildings may look impressive and the grounds may exude beauty and confidence, but the institutions of higher learning so often in today's world are tainted with the ideals of progressivism that lead to the shipwreck of many students who buy into these false and dangerous philosophies.*

Education, Computers, Humanism

Chapter 8

The University

From roots in Plato's dark deluded dream,
Sprang up one theocratic new regime,
So steeped in ice it knew not whence it came,
Nor limply sought excuse for sources lame.
What sources? Not at all must this world's mind,
Soon meet to reconvene the past's benign
And sordid refuse pile of thought stacked tall,
Now reaping full its catastrophic fall.

So here we stand, a people lost,
No place to run, no paths uncrossed.
One willy-nilly humdrum hive,
Of endless protoplasmic lives.

And here I sit within concrete and steel,
The whir and grind of man's machines so real.
No windows, no, just white cement-block walls,
And four gray desks, four chairs, cavernous hall.

The new and mighty, shiny works of man stand towering amidst the cold, shivery, bone-chilling north winter winds.
All new and bright, cold hulks rising from the prairie soil like cruel monsters, sucking in hapless victims careless enough to venture too close to their intellectual tentacles, to be thrust into the maw and digested beside the fleshly bones of countless other unwary, unblinking, unknowing victims.
Inside the monster's digestive system grinds out the produce of the world's intellectuals, whose resumes wax long and impressive across their desks.
Empathy was cast out before she ever entered; the monster never permitted her success.
Now pride has smothered all vestiges of humility (or so it seems for most), and the vestments have joined forces with self-appointed authority,
The beast's authors too self-exalted to extricate themselves from the worshipful temple of knowledge.

No Place for the Peace Lovers

No Inheritance Today

I have no home, no resting place for my head
In this darkened world, wherein I live in light.
I have no home or ranch of my own, no expanse of forest and meadow,
No cold mountain stream to caress my trail-worn feet.
Though a seed of Abraham, no claim do I lay this day to lands and wealth.
Yet, wealth I own, wife and children I possess, lands and homes I inhabit
That the Creator's great promises may find expression
Within this clay with which He works,
True wealth to mold rulers, kings, priests, and guardians
Of a world to come, when all kingdoms shall lay secure
Within their loving care and kindness,
While this deceived world failed to grant them power today over nations,
Power to heal and raise up, unrecognized dreams within darkness
Of the Adversary's falling realm.

No Place

A stranger in this place,
A sojourner foreign to this race,
Cast forth from society's moorings,
Not a part of this earthly realm,
But estranged from birth to be kept in waiting
For a Kingdom not yet extant,
A world, an eon still withholden
From mankind's view, for a season …
A short season.
Thus we of the unseen world wait,
Wait patiently for the fields to ripen,
For the wheat to turn golden and brittle,
Seeds supple in their glumes,
Pregnant to burst forth in harvest at the end.

Porter, Minnesota. *In this society it is quite impossible for a person to have a permanent claim upon a land that he loves and wishes to reserve for himself and his family. Land comes with a price in today's world, and titles can be transferred quickly and easily, so unlike the permanent tenure that our Israelite forefathers were given to their homesteads, which were to remain in the family forever.*

Chapter 9 No Place for the Peace Lovers

Unfulfilled

I strode upon packed snowbanks, over the snowy plateau of early springtime's
warming embrace,
In search of peace and solitude among the elms, boxelders, and willows
a short distance away
To view thickening buds, awaiting their burst to luscious, fragrant new life,
The grainy, glistening, dirty snow crunching crisply beneath my feet.

Yet, as I traversed the banks, gliding up one and down the next, I spied a jet con-trail high
above stretching white and rigid across the crystal blue sphere, cleaving it asunder.
I continued, crunching, hoping, seeking bits of green through thin barren patches
yet crusted with melting patchwork ice blending into melting drifts.
A hoard of migrating juncos fluttered noisily from their perches among the barren
limbs and branches.

Silence, SILENCE … where is it?

Suddenly the rumble of a freight train, plying the track a mile distant to the south, forced its
way into my senses, brutally seizing sanity with sickening clatters and hammering drones.
I circled back among the trees, through the caressing soft southwest breeze,
to view again the swelling elm buds, the rough clatter fading quickly,
As the acrid, pungent odor of diesel fumes carried by the lazy breeze reached my senses,
seeming to mock my journey.
Back toward home my footsteps plodded … heavier now.

Up the bank, down the slopes, drifts melting with springtime's mirth,
Patiently awaiting winter's retreat, to release captive life, to open bounds of expression
against the frigid sea.
One final insult plied the air: a low-flying airplane droned overhead … and I ducked
inside my home, as if in fright …
But no, in quiescent discontent, withholding of reward, insult of rationale.

I will wait.
I shall return.

Pritchett, Texas.
The appearance of condensation trails across the sky clashes with the purity of the created world, polluting the natural patterns that God created and placed in the heavens for the enjoyment and uplift of mankind.

Chapter 10 Traditions

Men Lost

Humanity lost, dumbfounded in fears,
Searching 'midst terrors life's comforting cheers;
Walking long corridors — sun blotted out —
Mingled with concrete and iron … and doubt
That man might unscramble his withering vine,
To cease lonesome battles, to praise bread and wine.

Humanity lost, its sun soon to set …
That new worlds may prosper through time's knotted net.

Paradigms

Perspectives deep within the mind retain their subtle grip,
Bequeathed through generations of our father's thoughtless slip.
Entrenched so deeply, time by time the paradigms grow strong,
As Eve's demise and Adam's slip envelop culture's throng.

Mexico. *The influence of church organizations on the traditions of men has been profound over the millennia, oftentimes casting the truth into the murky waters of syncretic deception, and changing the course of history towards wars and disruptions which have killed millions.*

Traditions

Vain Traditions

"Woe is the innocent hand of destiny, the flight of idle rote endeavor,
Bequeathed of tradition, fashioned of cloistered ancestors,
Handed from generation to generation, unknowing its heralded inception,
Nor acknowledging its accumulated dust of warped divinity through the musty ages.

"Woe is the innocent hand, that mortal visage of anchored posterity,
Embedded within ceaseless chants, bright days of endless sunshine and vineyards,
Rolling forever across waving, shimmering wheat and barley fields, seas of prairie grass;
Drinking the bitter nectar of fortune untended, garnered as if by mere chance, yet lying dormant, rotting, to no avail ...

> While heralding the coming gloomy skies prating
> A band of charioteers quickly gaiting
> Along the dimly-lit path of ages,
> Removed in time but strongly sifting sages.

"Woe is this hand, this leathery, tanned, wrinkled hand,
Seeking ever more accomplishment, triumph, serenity,
Striving valiantly against buffeting minds of the innocent hands about me,
Quivering in self-pity, agonizing in self-deceit.

> Oh merciless pain, when will your song
> Seek solace beyond the thundering throng
> Whose vain respects lie buried in this history,
> Which hauntingly clothes their lives in mystery?"

Continued on page 106

Miami, Florida.
Mankind's fetish for prideful expression, such as the towers and skyscrapers that hover over the cities and countryside of the world, seems to know no limits. The desire to dominate others rather than show love and kindness has translated into the hard and unforgiving nature of our Babylonian culture.

Chapter 10

Traditions

Continued from page 105

My knowledge ceased — as did wisdom and honor, judgment and mercy —
before the brilliantly shining face of my Master,
And in agony I struggled to collect my senses … and listen
To hope once again: yes, once again she spoke,
And I listened in obedient pensiveness,

Fighting madly to perceive deeper truth and passages
Amid the mediocrity of daily imprinting, abhorred messages
Flung round about on every side, stupefying — as it were — the perception
To proper thought, skilled direction.

Hurl aside the vain traditions, the folly of madness;
Seek deeper truths, the meat of things.
Recall the past as the deceiver's ungrateful fruit,
And proceed toward truth, rolling the past together as the great educator it is …

For in brilliance truth lies beside hope,
The faith of fathers long-since buried, who yet grope
In a vision, toward some ultimate great scene
Of pastures green, armies unneeded — utopian dream.

Continued on page 107

Traditions Chapter 10

Continued from page 106

"Past is past," I said, "and fathers have taught,
Mothers have tended through generations and generations,
As children grew to adult stature — adult mind — only to themselves bear children,
While the repugnant past meshed into future schemes …

As all were given the test
To see themselves, the impossibility of human success
Apart from the Creator, so clearly revealed
At every turn of history … so tightly sealed."

"Pick up yourself and walk once more," came kind, tender words
Across the soft, green, dewy meadows of my dreams.
"Past is past, but for you truth lies ahead.
Seek it, pursue it, bathe in it, be clothed with it."

So I sighed, and in hope continued again, more certain
Of the difficult road, stinging my feet beneath these burdens,
But the brilliant light at the end of the road so clearly seen,
Unhindered now by vain destiny — that fruitless, pointless dream.

Philippines. *Countless graves for American soldiers occupy military cemeteries in many nations, the result of failed efforts to reach peaceful agreements between nations. The governmentally mandated function of killing the soldiers and civilians of so-called enemy nations has haunted the archives of history since the beginning of this eon, when Cain murdered Abel.*

War and Self-Destruction

Contentment for a Season

Balmy spring days, cool nights, sunkist paintbrushes, shimmering daisies,
Warblers and bluejays singing joyously, south breezes swaying new-formed oak
and hickory leaves,
Greenery billowing skyward, shrouding enclaves in serenity and peace,
Men walking in harmony, seeking kindness, faithfulness, and humility …
Days of building gaining the ascendency, before summer's torrid
breakdown commences,
And wars of men wreak their havoc upon Jacob's land,
Laying waste the cosmos that this good earth so earnestly protected,
But now must be cast aside — Jacob's trouble to fulfill —
That millennial realms may again restore Eden to this bruised and darkened earth.

Senseless War

Strong men, lusty, tall, and fair,
Wielding sword with wild-eyed stare
Charging headlong into seas
Of seasoned soldiers, quaking knees
Primed to pay the warrior's price,
Life's last fearless sacrifice;
Hopes poured out on blood-stained soil,
Dreams cut short, a moment's toil
Of nation's lust that kings may gloat
'Midst borders large, war's threats remote.

Senseless schemes for vibrant youth
Stalk the lairs of fools uncouth;
Men fall down, nor shall they rise …
I cry … My brother, when shall lies
Release their clutch on men's pure guild,
That strong young men may not be killed
Upon the earth, their seed cast down
To never rise up from the ground?

No sense it makes; these men should live,
Raise families, build homes and give
The world a joyful legacy
Instead of silent vacancy,
Lost beneath the soil so still,
Nothing ventured, emptied will.
Only in an age to come
Shall strong young men yet see the sun.

Chapter 11 War and Self-Destruction

The Worst Enemy

Man ... his own worst enemy ...
Fashions tools to ease his labors:

> Plowshares to till,
> Autos to travel,
> Guns to hunt,
> Radios and televisions to communicate,
> And universities to educate.

Yet, in his vain strivings for ease,
This futile race yields a darkened utopia:

> Plowshares hammered into swords,
> Autos reshaped into vehicles of war,
> Guns aimed at brothers and sisters,
> Radios and televisions reverberating sins of drugs and rebellion,
> And universities teaching lawlessness and humanism.

Man's spirit allies itself with error,
Forsaking truth and her abundant glory
That rallies goodness, hope, love, and kindness
To forge each moment into joyful living,
Oneness with eternal spirit, prosperity and peace ...
Trusting not its own ideals,
Casting its own mortal self aside
In utter fear and agony
That man ... his own worst enemy ... will himself destroy.

Ukraine. *Nations have lauded the exploits of their military leaders for millennia, and memorialize these army generals in the most conspicuous places. There must be a better way to solve the differences between peoples than to go about destroying their young men and women in combat.*

Wealth, Money, Work

Hands Searching

Men walk facelessly to dead-end jobs,
Log time, sit in agony for the weekday to end,
Shuffling papers, fidgeting among intangibles,
Seeing no fruits of their labors, appendages of other men and machines.

The well-rounded man grows scarce,
Robots squeezed uncomfortably into compartments
For survival's sake,
Division of labor a new modern god
Of added grief, impersonal hopelessness
Slovenly dressed in business suits and bouncy flab.

Insanity it is,
Men craving to generate meaning with their hands,
Detached from fellow man through city streets and concrete facades,
Tethered from loving sacrifice — grasping for fulfillment but losing hold.
Insanity of insanities,
A world plunged into deep chasms of hopelessness,
Dark, scathing clouds of boiling madness
Of wayward minds guiding wayward subjects
Upon earth's heated desert plain of deceit.

Continued on page 114

Guatemala. *Happiness and fulfillment are seldom attained through the accumulation of wealth, for as soon as a degree of physical gain is achieved so many people look towards the next plateau of material gain, often to impress others or gain control over the lives of others. Serving one's neighbor with the wealth one accumulates is a goal that all men should strive for, in the footsteps of Abraham, a man rich in gold, silver, and livestock but richer yet in faith.*

Wealth, Money, Work

Continued from page 112

Masters of business search to further remove hands from their wares,
That feelings may not touch objects of love destined for fellow men.
These masters themselves yearn to escape their own prison,
fulfill themselves,
In boats, cottages, drugs, affairs,
Joy found not within new games they embolden others to play,
The less wary subtly lured into sequestered nets
Of society's faceless blunders …
Until seething masses of wayward, perverted, suffering souls
Rebel from this sacrifice of life where life never really was,
Slavery to release,
Hope to renew …
In search of new worlds they believe must lie somewhere,
Perhaps just out of reach, but somewhere … .

The Wealthy

The wealthy wax rich, their goods lie reclining,
Upon tables bare, amid slavery's sighing,
And Godly reproof strikes dumb ears inspired
To stifle the cries of young men ill and tired.

Viet Nam. *Kings and princes, the wealthy and the honored in this world, possess priceless things, such as this beautifully carved furniture set … and while wealth and material goods are not of themselves evil, placing one's heart and worth upon these material things above spiritual matters leads to disappointment and heartache.*

Zion

Beyond the Hill

In this world of hate and want, of quiet suffering,
I search each golden valley, on crests of hills I sing
Of worlds yet out of sight, beyond my hopeful look;
It is that unseen hill I seek, the one this world forsook.

The peaceful, winding stream I cross, on stepping-stones serene,
Striding through the valley's fertile bluestem, fresh and green.
At once my senses tell me "Stop! Your life may prosperous grow,"
But footsteps lead me up the rise towards western billow's glow.

The hill beyond I seek, contentment never sought
Upon this roughshod streamside ridge where vivid dreams are wrought;
To yonder rise in misty eve fond hopes as crystal lights
Beam forth that Zion's Mount I'll see … safe-guided to its heights.

High Atop Mount Zion

High atop Mount Zion I sit in splendorous passion,
Upon green carpets living, south breezes gently fashion
Their fragrant gifts of distant flower flung upon this rift,
Set aside for lonely few amidst a world adrift.

Continued on page 118

Jackson Hole, Wyoming. *Majestic mountains bring to mind, within the ancient memory of each of us, the mountain of God, where the Creator Himself resides along with His divine council. It is this heavenly New Jerusalem that all of the saints are looking forward to with unprecedented joy, when finally the earth will be administered not by the god of this world, but by the true God and the resurrected elect who will be working with Christ after His return … to return Eden to its fullness over the entire earth.*

Zion

Continued from page 117

The stratus grace a sky full-bent on dropping rain below,
Soils as black as midnight waiting patiently the flow
Of life renewed while for a season Babylon must feed
Upon their fertile provender that sap her herd and seed.

Mount Zion grants undying comforts, joyful meditation,
While all the world in pain convulses with greed's salutation;
From here life's dreams refocus whence they came and whence they go,
Redeeming lost path's resolution, castigating woes.

Up these steps I've climbed Mount Zion, in such awesome dread,
Nowhere else to go … no choice but to tread
The courses painful, toilsome, grievous with Your hand in mine,
Baring all, You search the heart, wiping tears sublime.

Mount Zion stands most beautiful, the joy of all the lands,
Atop the realms of all that is, of all that falls or stands.
Your solid fortress walls inspire me to that higher place
You have promised soon shall captivate the chosen race.

The sun breaks through the raindrops falling — light and rain, Your spirit
Washed in water, bathed in light we shall Your throne inherit
Within this Zion strong and mighty … I cannot grasp the vision
That awesome resurrection whence the flesh shall find revision.

This land I lost in former time, given to another,
But someday soon when Zion comes — my Savior and my Mother —
It shall be mine, a wondrous blessing to all earthly treasure,
Saved alive despite the doom of Babylon's dim pleasure.

The land upon which sits this soul seems live as holy ground;
Indeed its buried selfless passions lead me to its crown
Each year when hopes grow dim in lands removed from saintly sway …
Then here I come to God's own sun, to Zion's home to stay.

Morris, Minnesota. *A colorful lily seems to beckon the heavens to reach down and grace the earth with a foretaste of the justice, mercy, and faith that will define the coming age. The beauty of the soon-coming reality is beyond men's comprehension.*

www.ingramcontent.com/pod-product-compliance
Lightning Source LLC
Chambersburg PA
CBHW042012090426
42811CB00015B/1621

9780998025445